I0806733

Meditations on the Passion

The Way of the Cross

Published by Scepter Publishers, Inc.
info@scepterpublishers.org
www.scepterpublishers.org
800-322-8773
New York

Text and cover design by Rose Design

Printed in the United States of America

ISBN: 978-1-59417-243-4

Meditations on the Passion

The Way of the Cross

SUSANNA TAMARO

Scepter

Preface

I am particularly honored to write a brief preface to these meditations and prayers on the Way of the Cross, written with profound spiritual sensibility by Susanna Tamaro, to accompany those invited on Good Friday by the young people of Catholic Action to walk the streets of Trieste, Italy to their Cathedral. They will devoutly contemplate together the scandalous and revolutionary mystery of the death of God. But, with the Easter resurrection of the Lord—he who lives—death is defeated, and therefore life, suffering, and death are not rendered meaningless, but are completed and made full.

The mystery of God reveals to us, in the end, the death of death, which removes the most agonizing thought that can lodge itself in the heart of man: that everything that is eternal and true is not.

With surprising theological wisdom Susanno Tamaro shares the liberating and consoling mystery of the compassion of God. Theology teaches us that God cannot suffer, but he can *com-patire* ("suffer with") us. Why? Because God values man so greatly that he made himself flesh and blood to suffer with man, as revealed in the fourteen stations of the cross. "Hence, in all human suffering," wrote Benedict XVI in *Spe Salvi,* 39, "we are joined by one who experiences and carries that suffering *with* us; hence *consolatio* is present in all suffering, the consolation of God's compassionate love—and so the star of hope rises." From there, Susanno Tamaro helps us to discover that the Way of the Cross is, in reality, the way of consolation. It is the way of love. It is the way of life; the road of consolation and of love, the road of life.

—Gianpaolo Crepaldi,
Archbishop of Trieste

Opening Prayer

In the name of the Father, and of the Son, and of the Holy Spirit.

Response: Amen.

Lord Jesus Christ, St. Teresa Benedicta of the Cross said that the Church is a stream of pure water that flows through the centuries. In the short span of time that separates us from her words, man has managed to pollute every source of water: the seas, the rivers, the lakes, the polar ice caps. The origin and reason for our life has been transformed into muddy pools of poison. We have put ourselves in the place of the Creator. Without humility and wisdom, we thought we could control everything by following a life of domination and possession.

Therefore what should have quenched our thirst has become the beginning of our end. We do not know what a stream is anymore. We do not know what pure water is. We are not even able to feel homesick about it anymore.

Firmly convinced about the power of science, the new idol to which everyone is forced to bow down, we are certain that even this problem—this thirst of the world—will be resolved sooner or later. Yet we need only look around to understand that the thirst of the body and of the soul reflect each other. How many blank stares, how many lives without purpose, how much misery without words, how much space left to the great deceiver who rushes around grasping at everything?

We are thirsty! This is the cry that rises from the earth. The rich are thirsty. The poor are thirsty. The plants and animals are thirsty. The rocks and crystals are thirsty. The fire in the center of our little planet is thirsty. Even if we don't know it, we are thirsty for you, Lord, for your luminous grace.

For too long your Church has become an underground stream. Her dimension of salvation flows invisibly for most people. At times it seems that the Church prefers sugar water to the waters that truly satisfy our thirst. It prefers the weak light of a small electric lamp to the strength of the flame. The Church has also suffered because many of her ministers, instead of overflowing with the fullness of love, are bursting with ambition and a thirst for power. Because of this the sheepfold is now empty, and the flock has gone away. They wander aimlessly near the surrounding hills, without a shepherd and without a future.

Lord, transform us into tireless shepherds. May our faces be full of light—our words strong, our actions coherent. The spear that was thrust into your ribs caused blood and water to flow out: blood from your lungs, water that surrounded your heart.

Lord Jesus Christ, we need the greatness of your breath more than ever. We need your heart to become our heart; two physical realities and only one heartbeat. We need to remember in the deepest part of ourselves the wonderful freedom of being children of God.

S.P
O R
I
II
III

✝

FIRST STATION

Jesus Is Condemned to Death

V. We adore you, O Christ, and we bless you.

R. Because by your Holy Cross, you have redeemed the world.

Pilate said to them, "Then what shall I do with Jesus who is called Christ?" They all said, "Let him be crucified." And he said, "Why, what evil has he done?" But they shouted all the more, "Let him be crucified." Then he released for them Barabbas, and having scourged Jesus, delivered him to be crucified. (Matthew 27:22–23, 26)

MEDITATION

You are there in silence, already knowing the verdict. This same crowd one week earlier had surrounded you, singing hosannas. And now, in blind fury, the crowd only knows how to shout: "Crucify him!" The more Pilate hesitates, grasping at a glimmer of conscience, the more the crowd shouts all the louder: "Crucify him!" as one voice, as a roar that overtakes everything else. Instead of being thirsty for your words, the crowd is thirsty for your blood.

The crowd is made up of human beings, but it isn't human. The crowd is capable of doing anything. It shifts from one side to another in the space of a few seconds, like a weathervane driven by the wind. The crowd is a multitude, and the one who is a multitude acts quickly on the inside, transforming it into a stormy sea. Your face alights on the crowd, but the crowd does not rest its gaze on you. It does not do so because it can't meet the eyes of the Lamb, but because it doesn't want to. It does not do so because instead of shouting at you, it is shouting at the dark ghosts that pass through its soul.

PRAYER

Lord Jesus, the act of losing ourselves in digital communication tends to transform us all into a crowd. All it takes is one misleading word, one manipulated fact, to stoke the flames from one side of the earth to the other. The immediacy of the messages often overwhelms our conscience, dulling our common sense, going directly to our bowels, asking for the only thing that the lowest part of ourselves asks for: blood!

Help us to maintain the appropriate distance from these forms of communication, so that our conscience does not become dark, does not deliver us to the leader of the crowds.

Lord Jesus, whenever we are tempted to judge, remind us that it is not for us to condemn. Allow the gentle glance of the Lamb to become our only beacon.

ALL:
Our Father who art in heaven, hallowed be thy name. Thy kingdom come, thy will be done on earth as it is in heaven. Give us this day our daily bread and forgive us our trespasses as we forgive those who trespass against us. Lead us not into temptation but deliver us from evil.

At the Cross her station keeping, stood the mournful Mother weeping, close to Jesus at the last.

SECOND STATION

Jesus Carries His Cross

V. We adore you, O Christ, and we bless you.

R. Because by your Holy Cross, you have redeemed the world.

Then the soldiers of the governor took Jesus into the praetorium, and they gathered the whole battalion before him. And they stripped him and put a scarlet robe upon him, and plaiting a crown of thorns they put it on his head, and put a reed in his right hand. And kneeling before him they mocked him, saying, "Hail, King of the Jews!"

And they spat upon him, and took the reed and struck him on the head. And when they had mocked him, they stripped him of the robe, and put his own clothes on him, and led him away to crucify him. (Matthew 27:27–31)

MEDITATION

In the face of the unknown, of something we don't understand, it is easy to fall into the temptation to mock. You said you were a king. Instead you are nothing. If you were really a king, we would offer you our hypocritical respect. But you are not. To our worldly eyes, you didn't give any sign that you had any kind of power. You are just a body in our hands. Your fragility is offered to our basest instincts.

What joy to mock someone who, moments earlier, had assumed an undeserving title! You played with power, and now we are making fun of you. You can't play with power and her servants. Hail, king of the Jews! Hail, king who rides on a donkey. Hail, king without an army and without commands. Hail, king who remains silent instead of issuing threats.

PRAYER

Lord, in our time the way of power is a highway illuminated by neon lights, while the way of love is a path hidden in the brush. Many take the highway and few the path. It isn't wickedness, but a quiet habit. The highway is wider, more visible. There are more people there. The crowd obliterates every shadow. If so many come down this highway, one assumes it can't be all that bad. It is only by driving down the highway that a few realize how empty it really is, and how it destroys the will. I can only go forward. I go on, not by choice, but because of the compression of the crowd around me. Because of this, bitterness starts to take over my heart, little by little. The gall of cynicism invades my days. That which I don't understand, I look down upon. That which makes me feel unsettled, I scorn. Lord, the beatitudes belong to people who don't spend time with scorners. I pray that more and more of us will abandon the highway and search for the hidden paths. Give us a taste for risk and freedom. Enable us to always oppose the powers that crush humanity.

ALL:

Our Father who art in heaven, hallowed be thy name. Thy kingdom come, thy will be done on earth as it is in heaven. Give us this day our daily bread and forgive us our trespasses as we forgive those who trespass against us. Lead us not into temptation but deliver us from evil.

Through her heart, His sorrow sharing, all His bitter anguish bearing, now at length the sword has passed.

THIRD STATION

Jesus Falls for the First Time

V. We adore you, O Christ, and we bless you.

R. Because by your Holy Cross, you have redeemed the world.

Surely he has borne our griefs and carried our sorrows; yet we esteemed him stricken, smitten by God, and afflicted. But he was wounded for our transgressions, he was bruised for our iniquities; upon him was the chastisement that made us whole, and with his stripes we are healed. All we like sheep have gone astray; we have turned everyone to his own way; and the Lord has laid on him the iniquity of us all. (Isaiah 53:4–6)

MEDITATION

Now the climb begins—a climb that is really a descent. Jesus climbs toward Golgotha and descends under the weight of the cross. In a world in which the good has been reduced to what one likes and the bad to what one doesn't like, what sense can there be to such expressions, which are so far removed from daily life? To climb means to struggle. To descend—in this case, to crumble under the weight—implies a profound sense of humiliation. We live constantly immersed in a stubborn search for happiness. This is why we are here on this earth: to enjoy, to have no regrets. We demand happiness, and this pretense frames our days. Once we have abandoned the idea of God's providence to govern our lives, to descend fills us with indignation. Who would dare to ruin our plans?

The Prophet Isaiah says it well: "All we like sheep have gone astray; we have turned everyone to his own way" (Isaiah 53:6). But the road of sheep without a shepherd heads toward a cliff. Suddenly, right beneath our feet, the darkness of a disease opens wide, the emptiness of a loss, the mysterious shadow of death. It is there that we find God ready to attend to us. And it is Christ's destruction that allows us to become aware of the light in the deepest abyss.

PRAYER

Lord, the world you saved has slipped into predictable passiveness. The person has been transformed into the masses, and the masses move in an erratic way. The herd does not raise its gaze toward the horizon. It is content to continuously find new grazing fields. When both the good and bad have been destroyed, when the possibility to choose—in other words, that which makes us human—has been removed, what else remains? Only the ability to nibble, to consume, to await reluctantly the end of this spectacle to which we are have been called, without wanting it and without understanding its meaning.

Lord, the greatness of your sacrifice reawakens our hearts. It makes them flesh, not synthetic and artificial. Give us the awareness that within our hearts a great battle is being waged—and that only this battle, fought to the end, makes of man something great.

ALL:

Our Father who art in heaven, hallowed be thy name. Thy kingdom come, thy will be done on earth as it is in heaven. Give us this day our daily bread and forgive us our trespasses as we forgive those who trespass against us. Lead us not into temptation but deliver us from evil.

O how sad and sore distressed was that Mother, highly blest, of the sole-begotten One.

FOURTH STATION

Jesus Meets His Mother

V. We adore you, O Christ, and we bless you.

R. Because by your Holy Cross, you have redeemed the world.

. . . And Simeon blessed them and said to Mary his mother, "Behold, this child is set for the fall and rising of many in Israel, and for a sign that is spoken against (and a sword will pierce through your own soul also), that thoughts out of many hearts may be revealed."

And he went down with them and came to Nazareth, and was obedient to them; and his mother kept all these things in her heart. (Luke 2:34–35, 51)

MEDITATION

Mary is present. Mixed in with the crowd of curiosity seekers, she witnesses the agony of her son. She does not tear her hair out, she does not struggle, she does not yell. She is there to show her love, a love that, because of its depth, is exempt from any pretense. Among the living, there is no pain greater than that of a mother whose own son is torn away from her. It is unspeakable, unbearable. It is nature that rebels and overturns its own order. That little face, which for nine months she guarded in the shadow of her womb. She won't see him again. She won't hear his voice again, the voice that a long time ago timidly stuttered her name.

How strange Simeon's words must have sounded to the young mother who walked into the temple with her newborn baby. How many sleepless nights she must have "kept these things in her heart." The serene breathing of the baby in his crib and she, at his side, with eyes wide open, peering into the darkness of the night. "And a sword will pierce through your own soul also."

The sun, when it shines, does not really shine. The voice, when it sings, always stumbles on an out-of-tune note. Now, while the crowd pushes and strains so as not to miss even one second of the spectacle, she finally knows. The shadow has dissolved. It is in front of her, transformed in realty. The sword is unsheathed. The blood of the Son and the blood of the Mother are again united, as in the moment of birth.

PRAYER

Holy Mary, glorious Mother of all who live, look at these desolate times when the human being, more than anything else, is afraid of maternity. Turn your gaze upon us, full of mercy! Convinced that to have a child is a matter of technique and desire, many have forgotten the profound reality that conceals life within itself. The evil that corrodes us is not the sterility of the body, but of the heart. We want to be in control of everything. We demand, we claim—and we call this thirst for dominion love.

But as you teach us on the road to Golgotha, love does not expect. It is attentive. It does not run after. It welcomes. Love is sober and demanding, patient and merciful. Love generated from the depth of our being is always a sign of contradiction because it unveils the thoughts of the heart. It relentlessly separates that which is truly fertile from that which, following the way of manipulation, only pretends to be.

ALL:

Our Father who art in heaven, hallowed be thy name. Thy kingdom come, thy will be done on earth as it is in heaven. Give us this day our daily bread and forgive us our trespasses as we forgive those who trespass against us. Lead us not into temptation but deliver us from evil.

Christ above in torment hangs, she beneath beholds the pangs of her dying glorious Son.

FIFTH STATION

Jesus Is Helped by Simon of Cyrene to Carry the Cross

V. We adore you, O Christ, and we bless you.

R. Because by your Holy Cross, you have redeemed the world.

As they went out, they came upon a man of Cyrene, Simon by name; this man they compelled to carry his cross.

Then Jesus told his disciples, "If any man would come after me, let him deny himself and take up his cross and follow me." (Matthew 27:32; 16:24)

MEDITATION

How irritating! How many times do we have this thought during the course of our day? Suddenly our routine is interrupted by something unexpected, and this something forces us to come out of ourselves. This is what happened to the Cyrenean. He could already taste the peace he would feel upon arriving at home, when suddenly he is forced to shoulder the cross of condemnation. There is blood everywhere; flies buzz obsessively. The dark shadow of immanent death is already spreading over that poor, whipped body. This is the one who ruined the day! And it is not only one day.

Gasping for breath, dragging his feet, his hair transformed into cords of clotted blood. Who can forget him? The poor Cyrene farmer is sure that these images, along with the smell of desperation, the smell of fear—will haunt him for a long time to come. Nevertheless he accepts. He has to because of the soldiers. Brutal power is impossible to oppose. So they put on him the weight of the cross. He accepts out of fear. But that gesture of submission, apparently so humiliating, causes something to burst within him and open up a new, unexpected perspective.

PRAYER

Lord Jesus, habit is a great enemy of man's fullness. We distinguish what we like and don't like and with devotion, we follow the path traced by our ego. We aren't doing anything bad, we tell ourselves. And it is really like that—apparently there isn't any negative intention in the quiet succession of our days. But then the words of the Apocalypse come to mind: "If you are neither hot nor cold, I will vomit you out of my kingdom." The routine is unveiled from its hidden face of death, and then we understand your words. To be born into real life, we have to deny ourselves.

Lord Jesus, may we, in our daily lives, always say "yes" to all that ruins our minor plans. Open our hearts to the breath of the Holy Spirit, the secret guide of our days—breath of light, breath of wisdom, breath of fire.

ALL:

Our Father who art in heaven, hallowed be thy name. Thy kingdom come, thy will be done on earth as it is in heaven. Give us this day our daily bread and forgive us our trespasses as we forgive those who trespass against us. Lead us not into temptation but deliver us from evil.

Is there one who would not weep, whelmed in miseries so deep, Christ's dear Mother to behold?

SIXTH STATION

Veronica Dries the Face of Jesus

V. We adore you, O Christ, and we bless you.

R. Because by your Holy Cross, you have redeemed the world.

He had no form or comeliness that we should look at him, and no beauty that we should desire him. He was despised and rejected by men; a man of sorrows, and acquainted with grief; and as one from whom men hide their faces he was despised, and we esteemed him not. (Isaiah 53:2–3)

Thou hast said, "Seek ye my face." My heart says to thee, "Thy face, Lord, do I seek." Hide not thy face from me. Turn not thy servant away in anger, thou who hast been my help. Cast me not off, forsake me not, O God of my salvation! (Psalms 27:8–9)

MEDITATION

Veronica also is standing on the side of the road. She already knows Jesus. She had been following his teachings. Was she was a friend of the family, or did she find herself there by chance? We don't know. What we do know is that she is there, and she reacts the way all of us should react: immediately, without fear, freely, following only the voice deep in her heart. In our mind, the heart has been reduced to a pump. It breaks down and is repaired or replaced. When we really want live at a higher level, its terrain is transformed into a hunting ground by the arrows of love.

Veronica's episode opens our eyes to a different dimension of the heart. Her action is rich with maternity and compassion. It's doesn't come from a series of complex reasonings, but from a heart overflowing with love. Why is it overflowing? Because it contains more than that what it could humanly contain. The fullness of the heart and the search for the face of Christ are closely connected. Without looking for that face, the heart will more or less carry out its mission to pump; it will age within us, gradually beating less. Within us, it will eventually die.

"Look to him and you will be radiant," says the psalmist. The light of love present in every atom of creation flows from the face of Christ. It would also flow abundantly from us if we only had the courage to allow our hearts to gaze at him.

PRAYER

Lord Jesus, on judgment day, it will not be devotion, blamelessness, or beautiful speeches that will tip the scales—but love, only love. How many times we forget this truth! We fill the air with chatter. The louder the chatter, the more at ease we feel. We have spoken so much about God! But is this really what you want? Wit, hypocrisy, and intellectual acrobatics?

Lord Jesus, free your Church from idle chatter, from hearts barricaded by pride because of their own paltry knowledge, so full of itself. Give us the loving immediacy of Veronica. Give us a heart like hers that reaches out to others, welcomes them, rescues them without wanting anything in return. In front of every face devoured by suffering, may we always exclaim with certainty: "Yes, this is really a child of God!"

ALL:

Our Father who art in heaven, hallowed be thy name. Thy kingdom come, thy will be done on earth as it is in heaven. Give us this day our daily bread and forgive us our trespasses as we forgive those who trespass against us. Lead us not into temptation but deliver us from evil.

Can the human heart refrain from partaking in her pain, in that Mother's pain untold?

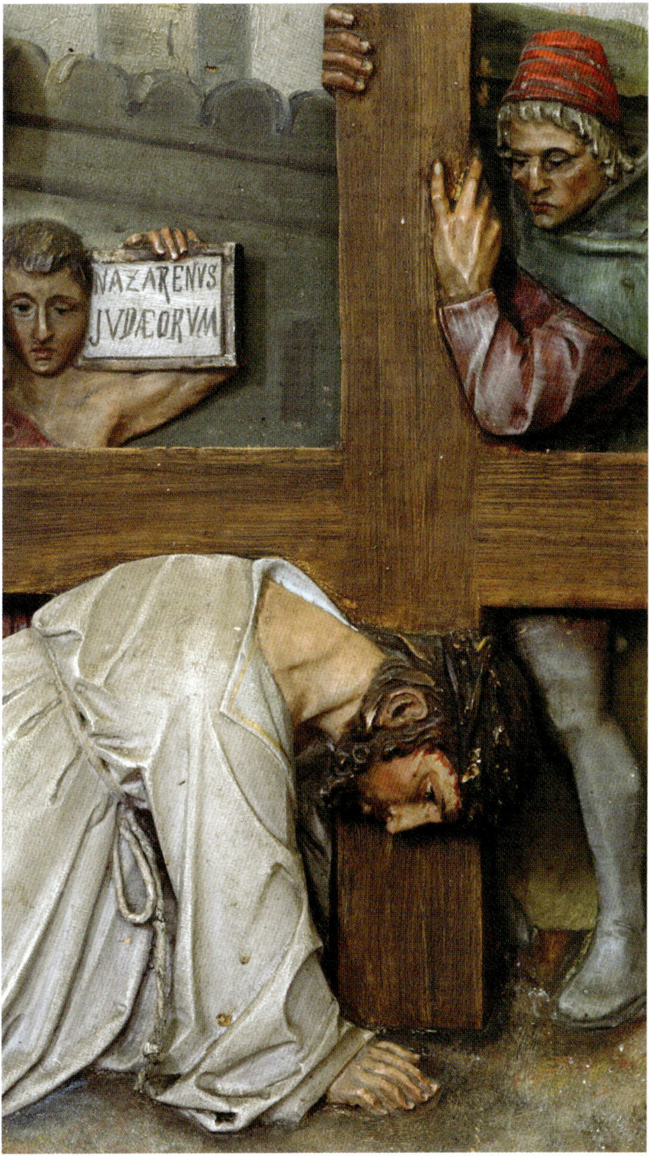
NAZARENVS
JVDÆORVM

SEVENTH STATION

Jesus Falls for the Second Time

V. We adore you, O Christ, and we bless you.

R. Because by your Holy Cross, you have redeemed the world.

I am the man who has seen affliction under the rod of his wrath. He has driven and brought me into darkness without any light. He has blocked my ways with hewn stones, he has made my paths crooked. He has made my teeth grind on gravel, and made me cower in ashes. (Lamentations 3:1–2, 9, 16)

MEDITATION

Jesus falls—and we fall, even though we aren't conscious of falling anymore. Adam fell—and we, continuing to fall, are convinced that we are still standing. We have removed the archaic idea of sin from our perspective, and what remains in us is an empty shell driven by the dark winds of convention. We are finally free, and this freedom has been transformed into something more terrible than a prison. But unless we fall, we can't get up. If we don't get lost in the shadows, we can't search for the light anymore.

We are born naturally good—this is what has been repeated to us over and over again, ad nauseam. Since we are good, we don't need anyone to teach us anything. We don't have to do anything, because our days are already suffused with the gentle aura of goodness. We only need to read the front page of any newspaper to understand how shaky this foundation is. Not even in the hearts of saints does goodness live undisturbed! Goodness is something to be fought for every day, every hour, every minute, and every second. It only takes a minor distraction for darkness to advance again. To walk is to fall and get up again, to fall again and get up once more. This is the true meaning hidden in the apparent banality of our days.

PRAYER

Lord Jesus, what is sin for us, if not the remnants of an archaic tyranny? Really, we don't know what to do anymore. Many of your priests, seduced by the siren call of psychology and sociology, don't even speak about sin anymore. Sin is a childish fantasy, a heavy-handed way to keep crowds in check in the past. We who have psychology, who read DNA-strands like a book, who have every type of pharmaceutical drug to regulate our moods no longer believe that sin is a basic part of our existence.

Lord Jesus, through the weight of the cross and your falls, help us to understand that to sin is more than missing the mark. It is the fragility of our own being suspended between two realities—heaven and earth. Sin exposes us constantly to this risk. May we always be conscious of the divine seed you have placed in our hearts that makes us capable of fighting in an untiring way to transform that seed into a plant. May it become a font of light to illuminate and give sustenance to many.

ALL:

Our Father who art in heaven, hallowed be thy name. Thy kingdom come, thy will be done on earth as it is in heaven. Give us this day our daily bread and forgive us our trespasses as we forgive those who trespass against us. Lead us not into temptation but deliver us from evil.

Bruised, derided, cursed, defiled, she beheld her tender Child all with bloody scourges rent.

EIGHTH STATION

Jesus Meets the Women of Jerusalem

V. We adore you, O Christ, and we bless you.

R. Because by your Holy Cross, you have redeemed the world.

But Jesus turning to them said, "Daughters of Jerusalem, do not weep for me, but weep for yourselves and for your children. For behold, the days are coming when they will say, 'Blessed are the barren, and the wombs that never bore, and the breasts that never gave suck!' Then they will begin to say to the mountains, 'Fall on us'; and to the hills, 'Cover us.' For if they do this when the wood is green, what will happen when it is dry?" (Luke 23:28–31)

MEDITATION

There are some well-loved phrases spoken by Jesus. Even people who are not familiar with him can easily repeat these verses without making mistakes. But there are other sayings—and not a few—that we prefer to keep in the shadows. They disturb us, and we don't want to be disturbed. We want to be soothed. When Jesus says, "I came to bring a sword," it frightens us. When he addresses the crying women who were following him by saying, "Women of Jerusalem, do not weep for me, but weep for yourselves and for your children!" his words bother us. Why launch such a threatening prophecy at those poor women? They were not making fun of him; they were participating in his pain with loud cries.

But the profoundness of Christ's gaze always discerns between what seems to be and what actually is. Conventional tears speak of an external pain, something for show. We release our emotions by crying. We feel better, and everything returns to normal afterward. This is not the way of conversion. This is not the way one embraces the cross. Faith never follows convention. It is always a rigorous search for the truth of the heart.

PRAYER

Lord Jesus, how many empty tears flood our days! We need only look at any television program to be overwhelmed. One cries about one's own misfortunes. One cries to be pitied. One cries to feel sorry for oneself. But there is no fertility in these tears, only the infantile debasement from something extremely important.

What are these tears if not a real and proper cleansing? A synthetic heart, a heart of stone, that suddenly discovers it is a heart of flesh—what then?

This heart does not run around making proclamations. It does not write theses. Simply, in silence, it abandons itself to tears. Before I did not see and now I see; therefore I cry.

Lord Jesus, forgive us for having fallen into the temptation of transforming ourselves into puppets that give in to our everyday ambitions.

Give us all abundant tears. May these tears wash away the incrustations around our hearts and our minds like a new and powerful baptism.

ALL:

Our Father who art in heaven, hallowed be thy name. Thy kingdom come, thy will be done on earth as it is in heaven. Give us this day our daily bread and forgive us our trespasses as we forgive those who trespass against us. Lead us not into temptation but deliver us from evil.

O thou Mother! fount of love! Touch my spirit from above, make my heart with thine accord.

NINTH STATION

Jesus Falls for the Third Time

V. We adore you, O Christ, and we bless you.

R. Because by your Holy Cross, you have redeemed the world.

It is good for a man that he bear the yoke in his youth. Let him sit alone in silence when he has laid it on him; let him put his mouth in the dust—there may yet be hope; let him give his cheek to the smiter, and be filled with insults. For the Lord will not cast off forever, but, though he cause grief, he will have compassion according to the abundance of his steadfast love. (Lamentations 3:37–32)

MEDITATION

It is hot. The road is long. The wood of the cross is heavy, and Jesus falls for the third time. Three times he falls. After three days he will rise. Three times Satan tempted him in the desert. Three persons in the Trinity. Three is the number of completion.

What is accomplished by this last fall? This fall challenges our obtuseness. We have learned to do without God, and we are sure that our independence will bring our world wonderful treasures. Thanks to our intelligence, we are already able to do truly extraordinary things. We no longer know what to do with rules imposed from on high. We have stepped on and laughed at the Ten Commandments. We have replaced them with our own laws. Technology permits us to manipulate life in all its forms, so why should we not believe that we are God?

And yet these wonderful treasures struggle to appear. There are a few rich people who are excessively rich, while the poor move like an irrepressible tide, an immense multitude dragging itself along. Twenty-seven million people survive in a state of total slavery. Human beings kidnap other human beings, selling them to the highest bidder. The ruling paganism too often reduces women to a mass of flesh. Flesh to use. Flesh to buy. Flesh to kill. Having decided to rule our own lives, we find ourselves in increasingly desolate places. Behind our lofty words of progress, we already perceive the sharp of fangs of *homo homini lupus* ("man is a wolf").

The deafening thud of Christ's body on the ground is like the sound of the trumpet prior to the judgment. Wake up! Open your eyes, open your ears, open your heart! Uncover the deception your adversary is plotting against you.

PRAYER

Lord Jesus, nature abhors a vacuum. We have cleared the heavens of the presence of the Father, and the heavens, instead of remaining clear, have been filled with idols. To them we prostrate ourselves, fooling ourselves into thinking we are free. The idol of money, the idol of power, the idol of sex, the idol of the right to happiness—these seemingly benign idols dominate our lives. What's wrong with wanting to be rich, seeking power, enjoying the pleasures of eros without limits? But inside their apparent benevolence, these idols conceal the leaden breath of death. Without your word, without your law, without your heart, the shadows advance, bringing us back to an indistinct and chaotic magma.

Lord Jesus, free us from a false liberty. Bring a holy fear of God back to our days. May the force of prophecy well up within us. May we always remember that he who does not love remains in death.

ALL:

Our Father who art in heaven, hallowed be thy name. Thy kingdom come, thy will be done on earth as it is in heaven. Give us this day our daily bread and forgive us our trespasses as we forgive those who trespass against us. Lead us not into temptation but deliver us from evil.

Make me feel as thou hast felt; make my soul to glow and melt with the love of Christ my Lord.

TENTH STATION

Jesus Is Stripped of His Garments

V. We adore you, O Christ, and we bless you.

R. Because by your Holy Cross, you have redeemed the world.

And when they came to a place called Golgotha (which means the place of a skull), they offered him wine to drink, mingled with gall; but when he tasted it, he would not drink it. And when they had crucified him, they divided his garments among them by casting lots; then they sat down and kept watch over him there. (Matthew 27:33–36)

MEDITATION

We all come into the world naked, but there are few that, in the moment of leaving, have maintained this nakedness. Adam realized that he was naked and felt ashamed when he was thrown out of paradise. The sudden nakedness of Adam is ours as well. But what kind of nakedness are we talking about? It is a little bit childish to believe that his embarrassment had to do with a lack of clothes. We have lost the clothing of glory; the splendor of God no longer enfolds us. Nothing, therefore, protects us from the weight of life and its wounds. Yet one only needs to look into the eyes of a newborn baby to realize that the dimension of eternity is still perfectly present. Then, however, the newborn baby will enter into his individual story. Others will clothe him; some clothes he will choose himself, until—little by little—his attire will be transformed into armor. The armor will allow him to be protected and stand straight, but it will not allow light to enter.

What, then, is the journey of faith, if not a continuous undressing, a determined search for that initial clothing of light? Jesus clearly indicated the path we are to follow: "If you don't become like children, you will not enter the kingdom of heaven." The path of innocence is the path of detachment and nakedness. To be tabernacles of light, we must become helpless. Only the pure heart is capable of shining brightly.

PRAYER

Lord Jesus, when I think about the agonizing nakedness of your body, I think about the six million Jews that, also naked, entered the gas chambers. In Europe that extermination opened wide the doors of paganism. When I think of your nakedness, I remember that 80 percent of all religious persecution in the world right now is directed toward Christians. Your Word always provokes hatred among those who love the shadows.

Lord Jesus, help us to support our brothers and sisters who live with persecution; teach us how we might share their pain. May we learn dignity and strength from them. Bring your Church back to the way of poverty. Give us the nakedness of innocence again, and the courage to always meet evil with a song in our hearts.

ALL:
Our Father who art in heaven, hallowed be thy name. Thy kingdom come, thy will be done on earth as it is in heaven. Give us this day our daily bread and forgive us our trespasses as we forgive those who trespass against us. Lead us not into temptation but deliver us from evil.

Holy Mother! pierce me through, in my heart each wound renew of my Savior crucified.

ELEVENTH STATION

Jesus Is Nailed to the Cross

V. We adore you, O Christ, and we bless you.

R. Because by your Holy Cross, you have redeemed the world.

And over his head they put the charge against him, which read, "This is Jesus the King of the Jews." Then two robbers were crucified with him, one on the right and one on the left. And those who passed by derided him, wagging their heads and saying, "You who would destroy the temple and build it in three days, save yourself! If you are the Son of God, come down from the cross." So also the chief priests, with the scribes and elders, mocked him, saying, "He saved others; he cannot save himself. He is the King of Israel; let him come down now from the cross, and we will believe in him. (Matthew 27:37–42)

MEDITATION

Now the crowd knows the truth. The one who fed the crowds, the one who promised them the world is basically a show-off. The game worked for a while, but now he reveals the lies smoldering underneath. "You who would destroy the temple and build it in three days, save yourself!" There isn't just mockery here; there is anger in their words. Many of those who were there had fooled themselves into believing that his words were real. Until the end they hoped for a sign that would leave everyone amazed. "Come down from the cross!"

If he had, everyone would have danced around him, singing praises! Instead nothing extraordinary happens. He remains on the cross with the two evildoers.

The logic of redemption is totally foreign to the logic of power. Where there is one, there cannot be the other. Only an immature faith makes us covet an extraordinary sign, something which permits us to tell others: "Did you see? Were you left speechless?" The only thing which is extraordinary is love. The entire universe is immersed in love, but we are not able to see it. The temptation of power always negates this vision.

PRAYER

Lord Jesus, you said, "I am the way, the truth, and the life." By not appealing to your divinity, you permit us to really believe it. By accepting pain, accepting death, you became the manliest of all men. On your shoulders you carry the entire weight of suffering of the world. You die, and we die with you. You rise and we, in you, have the possibility to rise. It is not an obligation—it is a door you opened with the great key of freedom.

Lord Jesus, moving away from the mystery of life has distanced us from the mystery of death. How much solitude, how much abandonment, how much desperation in the deaths of these times! The life according to the flesh leads to a dead end. Give us, therefore, the grace to stay near the dying, hold their hands, and accompany them like children toward the light of your glory.

ALL:
Our Father who art in heaven, hallowed be thy name. Thy kingdom come, thy will be done on earth as it is in heaven. Give us this day our daily bread and forgive us our trespasses as we forgive those who trespass against us. Lead us not into temptation but deliver us from evil.

Let me share with thee His pain, who for all my sins was slain, who for me in torments died.

TWELFTH STATION

JESUS DIES ON THE CROSS

V. We adore you, O Christ, and we bless you.

R. Because by your Holy Cross, you have redeemed the world.

Pilate also wrote a title and put it on the cross; it read, "Jesus of Nazareth, the King of the Jews." Many of the Jews read this title, for the place where Jesus was crucified was near the city; and it was written in Hebrew, in Latin, and in Greek. (John 19:19–20)

Now from the sixth hour there was darkness over all the land until the ninth hour. And about the ninth hour Jesus cried with a loud voice, "Eli, Eli, lama sabach-thani?" that is, "My God, my God, why hast thou forsaken me?" And some of the bystanders hearing it said, "This man is calling Elijah." And one of them at once ran and took a sponge, filled it with vinegar, and put it on a reed, and gave it to him to drink. But the others said, "Wait, let us see whether Elijah will come to save him." And Jesus cried again with a loud voice and yielded up his spirit. (Matthew 27:45–50)

MEDITATION

Now everyone is tired. The excitement of the preceding hours has yielded to exhaustion. Part of the crowd has abandoned the area. In reality, it was time for lunch. In the heat of midday, the flies are already depositing their eggs in the wounds, and the crows, attracted by the blood, flock in greater numbers around Golgotha. There is still time for sarcasm. "Call Elijah and let him come to save you!" The darkness that descended at an unusual hour has failed to frighten those present. Only when the shaking of the earth is added to the darkness does fear begin to grip many. The earthquakes signify the force of annihilation. That which we have built is destroyed in a few moments. It disappears and returns to indistinct matter. The sacrificial death of the Lamb brings us back to our absolute fragility. The earth shakes, and it rids itself of us. We thought we had the world in our hands, but instead it is the world that holds us in its grasp. Thus a tremor takes hold of those present, and spontaneously they say: "Truly, he is the son of God!"

Death is the only truly democratic reality of our life. It hits everyone without distinction and elicits feelings of fear and bewilderment in us all. The humanity of Christ embraces this until the end: "My God, my God, why have you abandoned me?" Instead of scandalizing us, these words bring comfort.

PRAYER

Lord Jesus, these times are as dark as the hours that accompanied your death. In reality there are not many who realize this because the artificial light more than accomplishes its task. The earth has taken note of our distance from the path of love. Instead of custodians, we have been transformed into destroyers. The degradation of the earth is nothing less than the projection of our interior degradation. The earth has a heart of fire, while in our heart your words have stopped burning. These two fires illuminate each other. When one is spent, the other explodes.

Lord Jesus, the entire creation is immersed in your love. Help us once again to perceive it. Help us to abandon the pathway of power and possession and pursue the path of astonishment. Help the ministers of your Church lead us to you—not across rivers of words but through the silent contemplation of the wonder of a flower.

ALL:
Our Father who art in heaven, hallowed be thy name. Thy kingdom come, thy will be done on earth as it is in heaven. Give us this day our daily bread and forgive us our trespasses as we forgive those who trespass against us. Lead us not into temptation but deliver us from evil.

For the sins of His own nation, saw Him hang in desolation, till His spirit forth He sent.

THIRTEENTH STATION

Jesus Is Taken Down from the Cross and Given to His Mother

V. We adore you, O Christ, and we bless you.

R. Because by your Holy Cross, you have redeemed the world.

When the centurion and those who were with him, keeping watch over Jesus, saw the earthquake and what took place, they were filled with awe, and said, "Truly this was the Son of God!" There were also many women there, looking on from afar, who had followed Jesus from Galilee, ministering to him. (Matthew 27:54–55)

MEDITATION

The scoffers have gone home. At the scene of the execution, only the women remain. They are not gossips; they are not fakes. These women walked with him for three years, eating his bread and his fish. They listened to his parables and decided to serve him. These are the women who were loved by him.

They never begged him to come down from the cross. They were not blinded by requests for the extraordinary. The fact that he died like all other human beings did not chip away at the trust and love that they still feel for him. They already know that daily life is the place where his exceptionality manifested itself. The women know instinctively that which is more difficult for men to understand. Except for John, all the disciples are in flight, while the women remained there. For the entire, unbearable length of Christ's agony, they never turned their attention away from his body. They stayed and waited humbly, in silence—so they could serve him one last time.

PRAYER

Lord Jesus, the Church in which your Spirit continues to live is a vessel nobody wants to enter anymore. Too much scandal; too much power; too much dull liturgical ugliness. Too many mouths that do not speak from the fullness of the heart. Too many eyes that are blind lanterns. Too much sloth; too much mundane careerism. Too much incapacity to speak to the desperate loneliness of contemporary man. Knowing how much you loved women, and how much the foundation of faith rests on maternal knees, it is fitting that they play a greater role in the Church. All of creation lives and throbs within this duality. The masculine and the feminine illuminate each other. When reality is tinted with only one color, it easily becomes sterile.

Lord Jesus, through the intercession of those women who attended you at the foot of the cross, help your Church to lose any fear of femininity so it can know how to open itself to this gender and welcome it, thus renewing the light of maternity.

ALL:
Our Father who art in heaven, hallowed be thy name. Thy kingdom come, thy will be done on earth as it is in heaven. Give us this day our daily bread and forgive us our trespasses as we forgive those who trespass against us. Lead us not into temptation but deliver us from evil.

Let me mingle tears with thee, mourning Him who mourned for me, all the days that I may live.

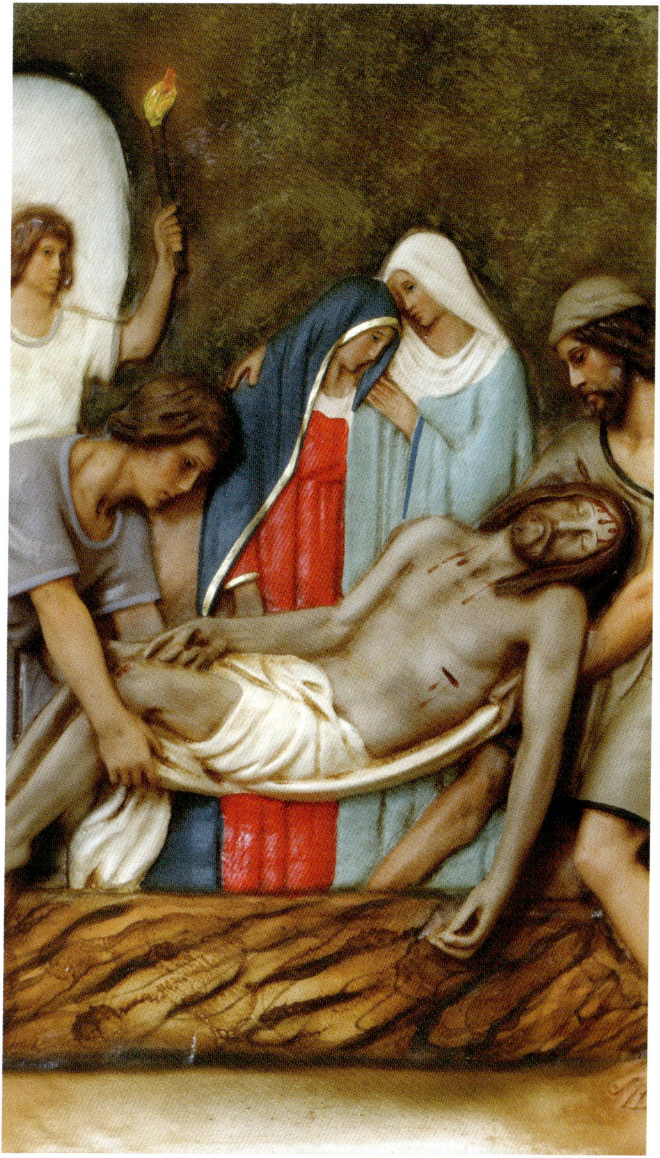

FOURTEENTH STATION

Jesus Is Deposited in the Sepulchre

V. We adore you, O Christ, and we bless you.

R. Because by your Holy Cross, you have redeemed the world.

And Joseph took the body, and wrapped it in a clean linen shroud, and laid it in his own new tomb, which he had hewn in the rock; and he rolled a great stone to the door of the tomb, and departed. Mary Magdalene and the other Mary were there, sitting opposite the sepulcher. (Matthew 27:59–61)

MEDITATION

Is there anything more terrible than seeing a loved one snatched by death? That which until recently was alive—and therefore in order—suddenly becomes disorder. Chaos wins, devouring before our eyes the face of the beloved. Joseph of Arimathea tries to bring dignity to the body. He anoints it, perfumes it. He wraps it in the shroud. Who knows if he is conscious that he is touching the mystery that underlies all creation? The grain of wheat is in his hands. The seed never dies; it is simply transformed. From that seed is born a plant. From the plant comes the wheat with which to make the bread. Here is the bread of eternal life, the bread of hope and salvation for all mankind. The stone rolls into place and removes from our eyes the instance when death is defeated. Once again we are not allowed to see the evidence of the extraordinary. We should not believe because of what we have seen with our eyes but by the evidence of the heart. "Were not our hearts burning within us?" his disciples asked after meeting him on the way to Emmaus.

The burning heart is the only testimony that is possible for us. Therefore, in the end, faith is this: a heart capable of setting fire to other hearts. Fires of hope, of love, of joy. Fires of redemption.

PRAYER

Lord Jesus, everything has been accomplished, and within our hands only bread remains. We are not always ready to understand and accept the upsetting simplicity of this mystery! Deep down it would be easier to believe in the manifestations of the extraordinary. Bread is a reality that is too ordinary and common to excite our imagination. And yet every time we draw near you, we know you are there. In the bread and wine, your victory over of death reverberates every second.

Lord Jesus, you have left us bread and wine so we can be witnesses of your concrete, everyday simplicity. You are with us until the end of the world. Help us to stay with you without hesitation, with the full knowledge that, from our first breath to our last, only your grace can cause love to burst into our days. Only the way of love can defeat death forever.

ALL:

Our Father who art in heaven, hallowed be thy name. Thy kingdom come, thy will be done on earth as it is in heaven. Give us this day our daily bread and forgive us our trespasses as we forgive those who trespass against us. Lead us not into temptation but deliver us from evil.

While my body here decays, may my soul Thy goodness praise, safe in paradise with Thee.

Amen.

Benediction

V. The Lord be with you.

R. And with your spirit.

V. Blessed be the name of the Lord.

R. Now and forever.

V. Our help is in the name of the Lord.

R. He created the heavens and the earth.

V. May Almighty God bless you in the name of the Father, and of the Son and of the Holy Spirit.

R. Amen.